Roald Dahl fans, rejoice at the opportunity to bring your favorite books and characters to life! Five of Dahl's hugely popular, beloved books have been adapted into winning plays for children. With useful tips on staging, props, and costumes, these plays can be produced with a minimum amount of resources and experience. You are sure to find these easy-to-perform plays a great source of entertainment!

ROALD DAHL'S

THE Twits:

A Set of Plays

ADAPTED BY DAVID WOOD

PUFFIN BOOKS
An Imprint of Penguin Group (USA)

PUFFIN BOOKS
Published by the Penguin Group
Penguin Group (USA) LLC
375 Hudson Street
New York, New York 10014

USA * Canada * UK * Ireland * Australia
New Zealand * India * South Africa * China

penguin.com
A Penguin Random House Company

First published in Great Britain by Puffin Books, a division of the Penguin Group, 2003
Published in the United States by Puffin Books,
a division of Penguin Young Readers Group, 2007

CIP Data is available.

Puffin Books ISBN 978-0-14-240793-6

PERFORMANCE RIGHTS: All rights whatsoever in these plays are strictly reserved,
and application for performance, etc., should be made before rehearsals commence to:
for amateur stage performances, Samuel French Inc., 45 West 25th Street, New York,
New York 10010; for all other performance rights, Casarotto Ramsey & Associates Ltd,
National House, 60 Wardour Street, London W1V 4ND.
No performances may be given unless a license has been obtained.
The publication of these plays does not necessarily indicate
their availability for performance.

Printed in the United States of America

7 9 10 8

CONTENTS

Foreword by Felicity Dahl   ix

Introduction by David Wood   xi

Meet the Twits   1

Meet the Muggle-Wumps   15

Skillywiggler and Spaghetti   29

Bird Pie Night   43

Upside Down Twits   55

The Dreaded Shrinks   99

Thank you, Bob Eaton and Jane Hytch of the Belgrade Theatre, Coventry, for originally commissioning me to adapt the full-length play *The Twits*; and thank you, Kathi Leahy, for directing such a splendid production which not only delighted the citizens of Coventry, but triumphantly toured the length and breadth of the UK and enjoyed a hugely successful season at Sadler's Wells Theatre in London. Your cast and production team brought the disgusting Twits to the stage with uncompromising flair and humour; your contribution is reflected in *The Twits: A Set of Plays*.

David Wood

FOREWORD

I am often asked if Roald based any of his characters on real people and I often answer that perhaps Mrs Twit was based on me. I hope not. I'm not sure I would have had the imagination she had in plotting her revenge on the beastly Mr Twit.

Roald was always worried about men with beards and would tease his friends who had them. He would say to me, 'Imagine the time they must spend keeping them clean. Do they shampoo after every meal?'

He also worried about men who paid too much attention to their appearance, especially men who constantly look at themselves in a mirror. As far as he was concerned, a mirror was to help you shave, brush your teeth and comb your hair. In fact, he rather enjoyed shaving and used to play a game every morning. He would try to shave his chin with three strokes and wondered why razors were not made in different sizes for different-sized faces.

I often wondered why he never ate spaghetti. Had someone once played a trick on him or was it just his imagination playing tricks? He disliked practical jokes and thought the people who played them were rather horrible. Adult practical jokes were the worst. Perhaps this is why he made Mr and Mrs Twit so horrible and gave them such a sticky end.

I'm sure you will have enormous fun performing these plays. Perhaps you can invent some of your own practical jokes for Mr and Mrs Twit.

Felicity Dahl

INTRODUCTION

The Twits, like most of Roald Dahl's books for children, is full of enjoyable theatricality. The over-the-top unpleasantness of Mr and Mrs Twit is balanced by a satisfying sense of justice as they get their come-uppance. The inventive storyline and colourful characters leap off the page and cry out to be put on the stage. Who else could devise a funny, moving tale involving an outrageously nasty married couple, a magical Roly-Poly Bird, an engaging family of Monkeys and a cheeky flight of Birds?

The first professional production of my adaptation of *The Twits* featured a team of local children playing the young Muggle-Wumps and the Birds. Watching the auditions, I was struck by the physical skills displayed by the children, most of whom had never acted before. Some showed remarkable acrobatic ability as Monkeys; others found witty ways of moving as Birds. All seemed to be thoroughly enjoying themselves. Why not, I thought, adapt the play for children to perform or read in class?

The advent of the Literacy Hour in the National Curriculum has led many teachers to use plays as well as stories. Plays encourage teamwork and a sense of community. Reading or acting out a character in a play is often more fun than reading out a paragraph from a book.

But a full-length play is perhaps too long to be explored in a lesson or performed as a school play. So I have divided the story into several short plays that stand up on their own. They vary in staging requirements and cast numbers. I hope you will have fun with them in drama groups and schools, whether acted out, read aloud in class or enjoyed at home. Roald Dahl was a great champion of literacy – his Foundation continues to support it. I hope he would approve of these plays and also forgive me for offering an alternative ending to his classic story!

David Wood

MEET THE TWITS

This play has been written for fourteen actors: Mr and Mrs Twit are introduced by twelve narrators. However, the narration could be divided between more or fewer actors if required. This scene would be an ideal introduction to acting out a story, preparing the group to tackle a more complex play.

CHARACTERS

For costume ideas, it is worth looking at Quentin Blake's memorable illustrations in the original book.

Mr Twit: he should wear long, unkempt hair, a dirty-looking beard and an ill-fitting shirt; his shoes should be easily removable, for speedy transfer to his knees!

Mrs Twit: carrying a walking stick and wearing a long, stained skirt and top; her hair is wild and spiky; she has a glass eye (see PROPS).

Twelve (or more, or less) actors: wearing their own clothes or a basic 'uniform' like jeans and T-shirts.

Two stage managers to set furniture: their jobs could be done by two of the actors.

A musician to play percussion instruments.

SETTING
An empty space.

PROPS
A small table and two chairs.

A small piece of green cheese and a sardine tail: these could be mimed.

Mrs Twit's walking stick: must be able to 'break' halfway down, perhaps one half plugs into the other half.

Two glasses of 'beer'.

Mrs Twit's glass eye: this could be a marble, hidden in her hand till she needs to 'remove' it.

An enormous mallet made of foam rubber.

SOUND EFFECTS
Percussion instruments as appropriate, especially drum rolls, musical 'pings' to accompany sudden ideas, and drumbeats for tension or to heighten the slapstick moments when the Twits hit each other or fall over.

LIGHTING
Nothing special is required, but it might be effective to brighten the lights when Mr and Mrs Twit make their first entrance.

MEET THE TWITS

Curtain up.

The CAST, *all except* MR *and* MRS TWIT, *assemble in a semicircle. Drum roll.*

ACTOR 1: They're shocking!

ACTOR 2: They're smelly!

ACTOR 3: They're silly!

ACTOR 4: They're stupefyingly stupid!

ACTOR 5: Get ready to meet . . .

ACTOR 6: The one and only . . .

ACTOR 7: Thank goodness!

ALL: The Twits!
   [*Fanfare*]

   [*The semicircle splits to admit* MR *and* MRS TWIT, *who enter with show-biz flair.* MRS TWIT *carries a walking stick. They act out the words of the* NARRATORS]

ACTOR 8: The best way to describe the Twits is . . .

ALL: Disgusting!

ACTOR 9: Mr Twit . . .
   [MR TWIT *steps forward*]

. . . was a very hairy-faced man.

ACTOR 10: His thick, spiky hair stuck out straight like the bristles of a nailbrush.

ACTOR 11: The stuff even sprouted in revolting tufts out of his nostrils and ear-holes.

MR TWIT: My hairiness . . .

ACTOR 12: . . . thought Mr Twit . . .

MR TWIT: . . . makes me look terrifically wise and grand!

ACTORS 1, 2, 3 and 4: But in truth he was neither of these things.

ACTORS 5, 6, 7 and 8: Mr Twit was a twit.

ACTORS 9, 10, 11 and 12: He was born a twit.

MRS TWIT: [*Coming forward*] And now, at the age of sixty, he's a bigger twit than ever!
[MR TWIT *looks angrily at* MRS TWIT]

ACTOR 1: How often, you may ask, did Mr Twit wash this bristly, nailbrushy face of his?

ACTOR 2: The answer is . . .

ALL: Never!

MR TWIT: [*Proudly*] Not even on Sundays!

ACTOR 3: As a result there were always hundreds of bits of old breakfasts . . .

ACTOR 4: . . . and lunches . . .

ACTOR 5: . . . and suppers . . .

ACTOR 6: . . . sticking to the hairs.
[MR TWIT *licks eagerly round his face*]

ACTOR 7: Specks of gravy!

ACTOR 8: Dried-up scrambled egg!

ACTOR 9: Spinach!

ACTOR 10: Tomato ketchup!

ACTOR 11: Fish fingers!

MR TWIT: [*With delight*] Minced chicken livers!

ACTOR 12: If you delved deeper still – hold your noses, ladies and gentlemen – you'd discover things that had been there for months and months.
[MR TWIT *delves in his beard and finds . . .*]

MR TWIT: A piece of maggoty green cheese! [*He eats it noisily*]

ACTOR 1: A mouldy old cornflake!
[MR TWIT *finds it and eats it*]

ACTOR 2: Or even . . .

MR TWIT: [*Digging it out*] . . . the slimy tail of a tinned sardine. [*He holds it aloft*]
[MRS TWIT *grabs it and eats it with delight*]

MRS TWIT: Mmmm. Tasty.

[MR TWIT *scowls at her*]

ACTOR 3: Mrs Twit was no better than her husband.

MR TWIT: You . . . you ugly old hag!
[MRS TWIT *reacts furiously, making herself look even uglier than usual*]

ACTOR 4: Ugly, yes.

ACTOR 5: But not born ugly.

ACTOR 6: When she was young, she had quite a pretty face.
[MRS TWIT *smiles 'prettily'*]

ACTOR 7: But she had ugly thoughts every day . . .

ACTOR 8: . . . of every week . . .

ACTOR 9: . . . of every year.

ACTOR 10: And so her face got uglier . . .

MR TWIT: . . . and uglier . . .

ACTOR 11: . . . and uglier . . .
[MRS TWIT *demonstrates*]

MR TWIT: So ugly I can hardly bear to look at it!
[MRS TWIT *scowls at* MR TWIT. *Then she hits him with her walking stick*]

Ow! [*He holds his arm up threateningly*]
[*Both freeze*]

ACTOR 12: Mr and Mrs Twit were a very happy couple.

ACTOR 1: But seldom happy at the same time!

ACTOR 2: For what really made them happy was . . .

ALL: . . . playing nasty tricks on one another!
[*A drum roll as* ACTORS *or* STAGE MANAGERS *position a small table and two chairs to one side of the acting area*]

[MR TWIT *unfreezes and tiptoes to* MRS TWIT, *putting his finger to his lips as if to tell the audience not to say anything. Unseen by* MRS TWIT, *he snaps off half of her walking stick. He hands it to an* ACTOR *or* STAGE MANAGER, *then takes, from another* ACTOR *or* STAGE MANAGER, *two glasses of beer. He sits at the table*]

MR TWIT: [*Warmly*] A glass of beer, my dear?
[MRS TWIT *unfreezes*]

MRS TWIT: Mmmm. Lovely. [*She goes to walk, using her stick, but it is so short she crashes to the floor*]
[MR TWIT *laughs*]

Aaaah! [*She struggles up, forced to stoop because of the short walking stick*] What's happened?
[MR TWIT *quickly removes his shoes, kneels down into them and shuffles towards her*]

MR TWIT: You seem to be growing, my sweet.

MRS TWIT: Growing?

MR TWIT: [*Arriving and looking shorter than her*] Growing. Take a look at your stick, you old goat, and see how much you've grown in comparison.

MRS TWIT: [*Looking at her stick in amazement*] Never!

MR TWIT: You always said you wanted me to look up to you! Your wish has been granted.

MRS TWIT: I don't want to grow!

MR TWIT: No?

MRS TWIT: No! Do something!

MR TWIT: Do something? Anything?

MRS TWIT: Anything! Stop me growing!

MR TWIT: Of course, my pet.
[MR TWIT *stands up, unseen by* MRS TWIT, *and fetches an enormous joke mallet, which he brings crashing down on her head*]

MRS TWIT: Aaah!
[MR TWIT *laughs and, seen by* MRS TWIT, *takes the bottom half of her walking stick from the* ACTOR *or* STAGE MANAGER *and replaces it*]

MR TWIT: Just a little joke, my honey-bunny!
[MRS TWIT *growls in fury. Both go to sit at the table and drink their beer.* MR TWIT *belches*]

ACTOR 3: Mrs Twit was determined to pay back Mr Twit.
[*Musical ping!* MRS TWIT *smiles*]

ACTOR 4: Suddenly she had an idea.
[MRS TWIT *checks that* MR TWIT *is not looking*]

ACTOR 5: Into her beer she dropped . . .
[MRS TWIT *pretends to remove her eye, revealing the glass eye (marble) and closing her real eye*]

ACTOR 6: . . . her glass eye . . .
[*A rhythmic drumbeat for tension.* MR TWIT *looks round with a hint of suspicion.* MRS TWIT *smiles innocently.* MR TWIT *drinks from his glass.* MRS TWIT *pretends to drink from hers. Then she pretends to notice something behind* MR TWIT. *He turns to follow her gaze. Quickly* MRS TWIT *swaps the two glasses round.* MR TWIT *turns back, suspicious.* MRS TWIT *drinks from his glass, he drinks from hers*]

MR TWIT: What are you plotting?

MRS TWIT: Me plotting? You're the rotter what plots. But I'm watching you. Oh, yes! [*Smugly she turns briefly away*]
[MR TWIT *quickly swaps the glasses round.* MRS TWIT *turns back, suspicious.* MR TWIT *drinks.* MRS TWIT *drinks, unsure of which glass she has.* MR TWIT *suddenly starts to sneeze*]

MR TWIT: Ah, ah, ah . . . [*He looks for a hanky but can't find one*] . . . tishoo!
[*While* MR TWIT *holds up his beard, sneezes into it, then wipes his nose on his sleeve,* MRS TWIT *quickly swaps round the glasses again.* MR TWIT *picks up his glass – in fact her glass – and starts to drink. The drumbeat builds*]

MRS TWIT: Oh, yes, I'm watching you like a wombat!

MR TWIT: [*Spraying her with beer as he talks*] Oh, do shut up, you old hag. [*He drains the glass and suddenly sees the glass eye at the bottom. The drumbeat stops.* MR TWIT *jumps with shock*] Aaaaah!
[MRS TWIT *cackles with laughter*]

MRS TWIT: I told you I was watching you! I've got eyes everywhere, so you'd better be careful! [*She retrieves the glass eye from the glass and holds it towards* MR TWIT *meaningfully, then replaces it in her eye-socket*]
[MR TWIT *roars and chases* MRS TWIT *round and round as the* ACTORS *narrate*]

ACTOR 7: They're shocking!

ACTOR 8: They're smelly!

ACTOR 9: They're silly!

ACTOR 10: They're stupefyingly stupid!

ACTOR 11: The one and only . . .

ACTOR 12: Thank goodness!

ALL: THE TWITS!

   [MR *and* MRS TWIT *take a bow, still fighting*]

[*Curtain down*]

MEET THE MUGGLE-WUMPS

This play gives young actors the chance to show off their physical skills playing Monkeys. It could be staged in the school gym, using ropes and wall-bars to climb on. The play contrasts the joyous freedom of the Muggle-Wumps' life at home in the rainforest with their humiliating caged existence as Mr Twit's circus performers. There are opportunities for actors of varied experience and enough roles for a whole class to take part.

CHARACTERS
Narrator

Mr Twit: wearing his suit and, in the rainforest, an explorer's hat; in the training scene he could remove his jacket to reveal a stained shirt and brightly coloured braces.

Mrs Twit: wearing her long skirt and top.

The Muggle-Wumps (Muggle-Wump, Mrs Muggle-Wump and their children, Muggle-Wumps 1, 2 and 3): their monkey costumes could be adapted from leotards and tights; in the training scene they should wear simple circus costumes – a tutu, a bolero jacket, just one item each.

Monkeys (the Muggle-Wumps' friends in the rain-forest): as many as required.

The Roly-Poly Bird: the actor can be male or female and should be dressed in colourful, exotic plumage; swinging on a rope to suggest flight would be effective.

SETTING
An empty space for the Twits' opening dialogue and the training scene.

The African rainforest, with colourful, exotic foliage, vines and trees.

A cage with bars and a door: this could be a simple cut-out structure either brought on for the scene or left permanently to one side of the acting area.

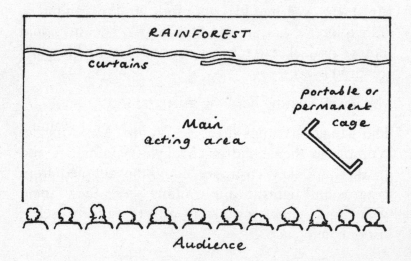

On a stage, the rainforest could at first be concealed behind curtains. The action could then spill downstage once the curtains are opened. Ideally the Monkeys should have ropes to climb, while the Roly-Poly Bird could 'fly' in on a rope and sometimes hover above the action.

PROPS
Mrs Twit's walking stick.

A banana.

A large net: this could be a large butterfly-style net or a big piece of netting.

The key to the cage door.

SOUND EFFECTS
In the rainforest scene, a recording of forest sounds, plus exciting live music and percussion could accompany the Monkeys' activity and the Roly-Poly Bird's entrance and dance.

Drumming and other percussion sounds could accompany the capture of the Monkeys and their training scene.

Circus music might be used when the Muggle-Wumps are dressed up.

LIGHTING

No special lighting is essential, but certain effects would be helpful:

- the general lighting could increase and become more colourful for the rainforest scene;

- the lighting could become more sinister for the Muggle-Wumps' capture;

- for the final 'moonlit' Muggle-Wump conversation, the general lighting state could fade down until only the cage is lit.

MEET THE MUGGLE-WUMPS

NARRATOR: Mr and Mrs Twit were a truly disgusting couple who enjoyed playing nasty tricks on one another. One night, when Mrs Twit was asleep, Mr Twit put a slimy frog under her bedclothes. To pay him back, Mrs Twit put squiggly worms in Mr Twit's spaghetti. But sometimes they had grander, even nastier ideas . . .

[*Curtain up, revealing* MR *and* MRS TWIT]

One day, Mr Twit announced . . .

MR TWIT: I've been thinking.

MRS TWIT: Did it hurt?

MR TWIT: I am going . . .

MRS TWIT: The further the better!

MR TWIT: I am going to run a circus!

MRS TWIT: To what, you twit?

MR TWIT: To run a circus!

MRS TWIT: Run a circus? You couldn't run an egg-and-spoon race.

MR TWIT: You wait, you old trout. [*Grandly*] I will train animals.

MRS TWIT: Animals, what animals?

MR TWIT: [*After a pause for thought*] Monkeys!

MRS TWIT: Monkeys? Where will you find monkeys?

MR TWIT: In the rainforests of deepest, darkest Africa!
[*Immediately, the scene changes. African drumbeats and rainforest sound effects play. Vines drop. We are in the rainforest*]

[*The* TWITS *exit*]

[*The* MUGGLE-WUMP *family and the other* MONKEYS *enter*]

[*Music can be heard as they play, climbing ropes and chasing one another. The* MUGGLE-WUMPS *establish themselves as a family unit. This is a scene of happiness and freedom*]

[*After a while, in flies the* ROLY-POLY BIRD *on a rope; or he appears above, on the branch of a tree; or he simply runs on*]

ROLY-POLY BIRD: Wheeeeeee!

MUGGLE-WUMP: It's the Roly-Poly Bird!

MRS MUGGLE-WUMP: Look, children, the Roly-Poly Bird!
[*The* MUGGLE-WUMPS *look up*]

ROLY-POLY BIRD: Morning, Muggle-Wump! Morning, Mrs Muggle-Wump! Morning, little Muggle-Wumps!

MUGGLE-WUMPS: Morning, Roly-Poly Bird!

ROLY-POLY BIRD: What a marvellous, magical morning!
[*Music plays as the* ROLY-POLY BIRD *flies or dances impressively, watched by the admiring* MUGGLE-WUMPS]

MUGGLE-WUMPS: Oooh! Aaaaah! Wheeee!
[*Unseen by the* MUGGLE-WUMPS, MR TWIT, *in an explorer's hat, enters. He sees the* MUGGLE-WUMPS *and rubs his hands in glee*]

[*The* ROLY-POLY BIRD *finishes his display and exits. The* MUGGLE-WUMPS *wave, then sit and rest.* MR TWIT *produces a banana and half unpeels it. He holds it out, then starts behaving like a monkey. A* LITTLE MUGGLE-WUMP *sees him. A drumbeat for tension sounds as* MR TWIT *tempts him with the banana. The* LITTLE MUGGLE-WUMP *advances. The others notice and react in an alarmed fashion. But the* LITTLE MUGGLE-WUMP *goes closer and closer and nibbles the banana. It tastes good.* MR TWIT *starts to dance a monkey dance. Jungle rhythms start. The* LITTLE MUGGLE-WUMP *happily joins in. One by one, all the* MUGGLE-WUMPS *approach and join in too. They dance happily, as if in a trance, circling* MR TWIT. *The other* MONKEYS *watch*]

[*Enter the* ROLY-POLY BIRD. *He watches, alarmed*]

[*The dance builds in intensity. Suddenly* MR TWIT *slips out of the circle, leaving the* MUGGLE-WUMPS *happily prancing. Then* MR TWIT *catches them all in a large net. (He either uses a huge butterfly net or throws netting over them.) The* MUGGLE-WUMPS *are trapped. They squeal and screech. The other* MONKEYS *react in fright and hide. The* ROLY-POLY BIRD *is concerned and flies or runs towards* MR TWIT, *who pushes him off*]

MR TWIT: Got you, my lovelies! You're mine, all mine! You're coming with me. To England! [*He starts to drag the* MUGGLE-WUMPS *away*]
[*The other* MONKEYS *emerge to watch and sadly wave*]

MUGGLE-WUMPS: [*Calling for help*] Roly-Poly Bird! Roly-Poly Bird!

ROLY-POLY BIRD: [*Calling after them*]
Be brave, Muggle-Wumps!
Tails up, heads high!
Come the spring, to you I'll fly!
Till then, goodbye my friends, goodbyyy-e!
[*The* ROLY-POLY BIRD *flies or runs off. The other* MONKEYS *exit. As* MR TWIT *drags the* MUGGLE-WUMPS *in a circle around the acting area, the scene changes back to an open space. They have returned to England*]

NARRATOR: Back in England, the Twits prepared the Muggle-Wumps for work.

[*Circus-style music as* MRS TWIT *joins* MR TWIT]

[*They remove the net and the* MUGGLE-WUMPS *cower in a clump. Each is pulled from the group to be quickly dressed in a simple costume — a tutu or a bolero jacket or a hat. They are totally dejected*]

[*As they dress the* MUGGLE-WUMPS, MR *and* MRS TWIT *use brief commands or encouragements, a mixture of uncompromising harshness and twee, patronizing praise. For example:*]

MR and MRS TWIT:
Arms up! Arms in! Pretty monkey!
Stay still! Turn round! In! On!
Clever, clever! That's it, my lovely!
What a good monkey!
Don't move till I tell you!
Up! Turn! Arm! Leg!
Handsome as a human. Nearly.
Don't you look sweety-weety, cutesy-wutesy!
Aaah! Pretty little monkey-person.

[*The music continues as* MR TWIT *tries to force the* MUGGLE-WUMPS *to perform. He uses* MRS TWIT's *stick to prod them into rolling head over heels or jumping in the air. He shouts short, sharp instructions. For example:*]

MR TWIT:
Up!
Down!

Stay!
Over!
Jump!
Back!
Roll!
Go!
Turn!

[*But the* MUGGLE-WUMPS *resist. They poke out their tongues and pull faces at* MR TWIT, *who grows increasingly frustrated and cross*]

[MRS TWIT *watches, unimpressed by* MR TWIT's *efforts*]

[*Finally* MR TWIT *gives up. Music continues as he and* MRS TWIT *drag a large cage on to one side of the stage and, prodding with* MRS TWIT's *stick, force the* MUGGLE-WUMPS *to enter it.* MR TWIT *locks the cage with a large key. The* TWITS *exit as the lighting fades to night-time. Moonlight illuminates the cage. The* MUGGLE-WUMPS *are huddled up inside*]

LITTLE MUGGLE-WUMP 1: Mum?

MRS MUGGLE-WUMP: Yes, dear?

LITTLE MUGGLE-WUMP 1: This place stinks.

MRS MUGGLE-WUMP: Yes, dear. Go to sleep.
[*Pause*]

LITTLE MUGGLE-WUMP 2: Dad?

MUGGLE-WUMP: Yes, son?

LITTLE MUGGLE-WUMP 2: I want to go home.

MUGGLE-WUMP: We'd all like to go home, son. Go to sleep.
[*Pause*]

LITTLE MUGGLE-WUMP 3: Mum?

MRS MUGGLE-WUMP: Yes, dear?

LITTLE MUGGLE-WUMP 3: I'm cold.

MRS MUGGLE-WUMP: Cuddle up to me and go to sleep.
[*Pause*]

LITTLE MUGGLE-WUMP 1: Dad?

MUGGLE-WUMP: Yes?

LITTLE MUGGLE-WUMP 1: Tell us a story.

MUGGLE-WUMP: Well . . .

LITTLE MUGGLE-WUMPS: Please!

MUGGLE-WUMP: All right. Once upon a time, there was a friendly forest in a beautiful far-off land. In the tall, sweet-smelling trees a family of monkeys played, and every day their friend the Roly-Poly Bird came to say hello. And they were all happy.
[*Pause*]

LITTLE MUGGLE-WUMP 1: Is that it?

MUGGLE-WUMP: That's it.

LITTLE MUGGLE-WUMP I: [*With a yawn*] It's a nice
story.

[*The* MUGGLE-WUMPS *prepare to sleep as the lighting
fades*]

[*Curtain down*]

SKILLYWIGGLER AND SPAGHETTI

A narrator introduces this play, which provides two starring comedy roles for Mr and Mrs Twit. It requires energetic, extrovert character acting and would be an ideal entry for a one-act-play festival or a drama exam.

CHARACTERS
Narrator

Mr Twit: at first he wears a funny, grubby nightshirt; then he should change into his ill-fitting suit, with or without his jacket.

Mrs Twit: at first she wears a funny nightdress and curlers in her hair; then she should put on an apron.

SETTING
An empty space in which stands:

• the Twits' bed;

• a cooking stove and worktop.

It is suggested that the bed should stand upright, as either a cut-out behind which the Twits stand or as a portable truck with back and front – headboard and bedcover – between which the Twits stand. The cooking stove and worktop can be set behind the bed,

Front View

Bedsheet

wheels

Side View

Stove/
worktop

ready to be revealed later, or attached to the back of the bed, which could revolve to reveal them.

A small table and two chairs: they start off to one side of the stage.

Some rocks or stones at the edge of the stage. Behind or under them are hidden the frog and the worms.

PROPS
A glass of water.

A large, slimy-looking frog.

A second, identical frog, attached to a stick so that Mrs Twit can manipulate it under the bedclothes and make it jump on her face.

A saucepan.

Tablecloth and cutlery.

Spaghetti.

Several squiggly worms: the rubber kind you can buy in a joke shop.

Two bowls: one of them could have a section of its base removed to allow Mr Twit's unseen hand to make the spaghetti squirm and heave.

A cheese dispenser.

A sauce bottle.

A dinner gong and beater.

SOUND EFFECTS AND LIGHTING
No special sound or lighting is required.

SKILLYWIGGLER AND SPAGHETTI

NARRATOR: The disgusting Mr and Mrs Twit like nothing more than playing nasty tricks on one another. But today Mr Twit has been trying, with not much success, to train monkeys for the circus he hopes to run. Now it's time for bed.
[*Curtain up*]

[MR *and* MRS TWIT *enter from opposite sides. They are wearing funny, dirty night attire. They get into the bed, centre stage*]

MRS TWIT: Them blooming monkeys are a waste of space.

MR TWIT: Shut up, fungus face.

MRS TWIT: A load of woolly wallies, that's all they are.

MR TWIT: That's all you know, camel-breath.

MRS TWIT: All I know is, you'll never train them chattering charlies.

MR TWIT: Yes, I will!

MRS TWIT: No, you won't!

MR TWIT: I will!

MRS TWIT: You won't!

MR TWIT: Will!

MRS TWIT: Won't!

MR TWIT: Will!

MRS TWIT: Won't!

MR TWIT: Won't!

MRS TWIT: Will!

MR TWIT: Hah! Gotcha! [*He gets out of bed*]

MRS TWIT: Where are you off to?

MR TWIT: I want a drink.

MRS TWIT: You want a brain. [*She laughs heartily, then dozes off, snoring gently*]
    [*The* NARRATOR *hands* MR TWIT *a glass of water. He starts to drink*]

NARRATOR: Mr Twit was reminded of the time when Mrs Twit had dropped her glass eye in his glass of beer. As he drank he had suddenly seen the eye staring at him . . .

MR TWIT: [*Remembering*] Aaaah!

NARRATOR: He decided to pay Mrs Twit back.
    [MR TWIT *reaches into his beard and brings out a large, slimy frog. Alternatively, he goes 'outside' and finds it under the stones*]

MR TWIT: Come on, fat froggy, do your slimy, grimy worst! [*Smiling in anticipation, he tiptoes over to the bed and slips the frog under the sheet near* MRS TWIT*'s feet*] [*Pause*]

[MR TWIT *watches as the shape of the frog moves under the sheet. In fact,* MRS TWIT *is manipulating the 'frog on a stick' under the sheet*]

MRS TWIT: [*Suddenly*] Aaaaaah! [*She bounces about*]

MR TWIT: What's the matter, light of my life?

MRS TWIT: Help! There's something in the bed!

MR TWIT: I'll bet it's that Giant Skillywiggler!

MRS TWIT: What Skigglewilly? Ah! It's all slimy!

MR TWIT: The Giant Skillywiggler that jumped out of my suitcase when I got home from Africa.

MRS TWIT: Never!

MR TWIT: Yes. I tried to kill it, but it got away. It disappeared under a pile of your knickers!

MRS TWIT: Help! Save me! It's crawling on my feet!

MR TWIT: It's got teeth like screwdrivers.

MRS TWIT: Aaaah!

MR TWIT: It'll bite off your toes!

MRS TWIT: Aaaah!

MR TWIT: And nibble your knees!

MRS TWIT: Aaaaaaaah! It's tickling my tummy!
　　[MR TWIT *pulls the sheet down a little. The frog jumps up on to* MRS TWIT*'s face*]

My nose! My nose!
　　[MR TWIT *grabs the frog and holds it up*]

MR TWIT: By golly, it *is* a Giant Skillywiggler!

MRS TWIT: Aaaah! [*She faints*]
　　[MR TWIT *laughs heartily, then throws the glass of water in* MRS TWIT*'s face. She comes to with a splutter*]

[*Shouting*]

You scrabby old scumbag!
You sneaky old snake!
You scheming old scallop!
You wait! You wait!
　　[MRS TWIT *chases* MR TWIT *off*]

　　[*The* NARRATOR *moves the bed or turns it round, revealing a stove with a saucepan on the hob. Then he positions the table and chairs further downstage*]

NARRATOR: Mrs Twit, as you might expect, did not forget about her husband's Giant Skillywiggler joke. Next day, at lunchtime, she decided to pay him back.

[*Enter* MRS TWIT, *wearing an apron. She goes to the stove. She sings innocently as she picks up the saucepan*]

MRS TWIT: La, la, la, la, la, la, laaaa! [*Calling*] My dearest! Why don't I make us each a nice, mouth-watering bowl of spaghetti? Eh?

MR TWIT: [*Entering, no longer wearing his night attire*] Mmm. Yes. Why not, my little dumpling? Good idea. Spaghetti. I like spaghetti.
[MR TWIT *starts to la-la a romantic Italian tune as he lays the table with cloth and cutlery. Meanwhile,* MRS TWIT *puts spaghetti in the saucepan*]

[*Then, unseen by* MR TWIT, MRS TWIT *goes 'outside' and finds some squiggly, squirming worms. She smiles as she drops them into her apron pocket, then returns to the stove, joining in* MR TWIT*'s singing*]

[MR TWIT *sits at the table. He takes off his shoes, revealing holey socks, wriggles his toes and, leaning back, nods off to sleep. His singing turns into snoring*]

[MRS TWIT *continues to sing happily as she finishes cooking. She serves up the spaghetti, dividing it between two bowls and sprinkling cheese and sauce on top. She gleefully adds the worms to* MR TWIT*'s bowl. She brings the bowls to the table, then returns to find a dinner gong, which she holds very close to the sleeping* MR TWIT*'s ear and bangs very loudly.* MR TWIT *wakes with a start and nearly falls off his chair*]

MRS TWIT: [*Sweetly*] Your spaghetti, my dreamboat, my dove!

MR TWIT: Mmm. Scrummy. [*He picks up his fork and goes to take some spaghetti*]
[*Meanwhile,* MRS TWIT *tucks into hers*]

Hey, my spaghetti is moving.

MRS TWIT: What's that, my angel-puss?

MR TWIT: It's all squirmy. [*He holds up the bowl. The spaghetti is moving*]

MRS TWIT: It's a new kind. It's called Squiggly Spaghetti. It's delicious. Eat it up while it's nice and hot.
[MR TWIT *starts to tuck in, forking up the spaghetti and shovelling it into his mouth, slurping and leaving a mess on his beard.* MRS TWIT *watches eagerly*]

MR TWIT: [*Chewing hard*] It's not as good as the ordinary kind. It's too squishy.

MRS TWIT: Oh? I find it very tasty.

MR TWIT: [*Swallowing a mouthful*] I find it rather bitter. It's got a distinctly bitter flavour. Buy the other kind next time. [*But he goes on eating, with the occasional burp*]
[MRS TWIT *can hardly contain her delight. As he finishes his plateful . . .*]

MRS TWIT: You want to know why your spaghetti was squirmy and squishy?

MR TWIT: [*Wiping his mouth on the tablecloth*] Why?

MRS TWIT: And why it had a nasty bitter taste?

MR TWIT: Why?

MRS TWIT: Because it was worms! [*She roars with laughter*] Because it was WORMS!
[MR TWIT *clutches his throat in sickly horror. Then he howls at* MRS TWIT *and chases her round the table and off the stage*]

[*Curtain down*]

BIRD PIE NIGHT

This play offers opportunities for mime and move-
ment. There is considerable humour, but the predica-
ment of the Muggle-Wumps and the danger posed to
the Birds make it sinister and moving too. A narrator
helps to tell the story.

CHARACTERS
Narrator

Mr Twit: wearing his explorer's hat and his ill-fitting
suit, or long khaki shorts.

Mrs Twit: wearing her long skirt and top.

The Muggle-Wumps (Muggle-Wump, Mrs Muggle-
Wump and their children, Muggle-Wumps 1, 2 and
3): they should wear monkey costumes, plus their
simple circus outfits.

The Birds (several puppeteers carrying birds on poles
—either single birds or a 'spray' of several birds): the
puppeteers could be dressed in jeans and T-shirts or
in bird costumes.

Flight of birds

made by fixing
cut-outs to
straightened-out
coathanger wire
attached to a pole

SETTING

In an otherwise empty space are:

• the Muggle-Wumps' barred cage, which could be a simple cut-out—the door could be imagined;

• the Big Dead Tree, which could also be a cut-out, with several branches for the Birds to perch on.

Ideally the cage and the tree would at first be hidden from view by curtains.

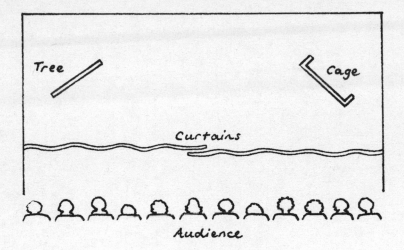

PROPS
Mrs Twit's walking stick.

The key to the cage door.

A bowl of bananas for the Muggle-Wumps.

A large net on a long pole.

SOUND EFFECTS AND LIGHTING
No special sound or lighting is required, but it would be effective if music could accompany the entrance of the Birds and if tension music, perhaps a drumbeat pulse, could punctuate the Twits' attempted capture of the Birds.

BIRD PIE NIGHT

If there are curtains, the play begins in front of them.

NARRATOR: The extremely unpleasant Mr Twit . . .
   [MR TWIT *enters with a stick and poses like a big-game hunter*]

. . . goes to the rainforest of Africa and catches a family of monkeys, the Muggle-Wumps.
   [*The* MUGGLE-WUMPS *enter, animated and bright.* MR TWIT *gestures threateningly and they cower, frightened*]

He brings them back to England, where he will train them to appear in his Monkey Circus.
   [MR TWIT *gestures and the* MUGGLE-WUMPS *take up a circus pose*]

The equally extremely unpleasant Mrs Twit . . .
   [MRS TWIT *enters, grabs the stick and threatens* MR TWIT *with it. They both freeze*]

. . . helps him lock the Muggle-Wumps . . .
   [*Curtain up*]

   [*The cage and the Big Dead Tree are revealed*]

. . . inside a cage.
   [MR *and* MRS TWIT *drive the* MUGGLE-WUMPS *towards the cage and push them inside, then* MR TWIT

locks the door. He takes the key and MR *and* MRS TWIT
exit. The MUGGLE-WUMPS *relax*]

Near the cage stood the Big Dead Tree.
[*The* NARRATOR *indicates the tree*]

Every evening, as the sun went down, birds would
fly in from all around to roost for the night on its
branches.
[*Music as the* BIRDS *enter and fly in formation around
the stage—a short choreographed sequence*]

On one particular evening, as the Muggle-Wumps
relaxed after a hard day's training . . .
[*The* MUGGLE-WUMPS *stir in the cage*]

LITTLE MUGGLE-WUMP 1: Hey, Mum, Dad!

LITTLE MUGGLE-WUMP 2: Look!

LITTLE MUGGLE-WUMP 3: Look at the birds!
[*The* MUGGLE-WUMPS *watch as the* BIRDS *continue
to fly round. Eventually they land and settle on the branches
of the tree*]

[MR *and* MRS TWIT *enter with a bowl of bananas for
the* MUGGLE-WUMPS]

MR TWIT: Come and get it, my lovelies. Grub up!
[*He opens the cage with the key and pushes in the bowl of
bananas*]
[*The* MUGGLE-WUMPS *press round and start feeding*]

MRS TWIT: They're eating us out of house and home, them greedy guzzlers.

MR TWIT: Got to feed 'em up. Build up their strength. They'll never perform on empty stomachs.

MRS TWIT: They'll never perform full stop. Mangy mugginses. [*She prods them with her stick. To the* MUGGLE-WUMPS] That's my supper you're stuffing!

MR TWIT: Shut up moaning. Come the day they make us rich and famous, you'll have caviar and champagne.

MRS TWIT: If I haven't starved to death in the mean-time. [*She sees the* BIRDS] Oh, look, the blooming birds are back. I hate them, messy creatures. [*She advances with her stick*] Clear off . . .

MR TWIT: [*Stopping her*] Wait, wait! [*He points at the* BIRDS] Supper!

MRS TWIT: Eh?

MR TWIT: Tasty, toothsome, tickle your palate . . . Bird Pie!
  [MRS TWIT*'s eyes light up*]
Shhhh!
  [MR *and* MRS TWIT *creep backwards, not wanting to disturb the* BIRDS, *then exit. The* MUGGLE-WUMPS *watch them as they go*]

LITTLE MUGGLE-WUMP 1: Mum!

LITTLE MUGGLE-WUMP 2: Dad!

LITTLE MUGGLE-WUMP 3: What's going on?

MRS MUGGLE-WUMP: Shh! Something to do with the birds.

LITTLE MUGGLE-WUMP 1: Don't they like them?

MUGGLE-WUMP: Oh, yes, son. I think they like them a lot . . .
[*The* TWITS *enter with a large net on a long pole. They gingerly approach the tree*]

MR TWIT: [*Grabbing the net*] I'll do it!

MRS TWIT: [*Grabbing the net*] I'll do it!

MR TWIT: [*Grabbing the net*] I'll do it!

MRS TWIT: [*Grabbing the net*] I'll do it!

MR and MRS TWIT: [*Together*] Oh, all right, then. You do it!
[*They drop the net with a clatter. The* BIRDS *stir, but settle again*]

MR and MRS TWIT: [*Together*] Shhh!
[MR TWIT *grabs the net and slowly advances.* MRS TWIT *pushes him*]

MRS TWIT: Go on.

MR TWIT: Shut up! [*He turns, swinging the net, hitting* MRS TWIT]

MRS TWIT: Ow!

MR TWIT: Shut up! [*He swings back. The net hits* MRS TWIT *again*]

MRS TWIT: Ow!

MR TWIT: Shhh!
[*They start off again. Suddenly . . .*]

Now! [*He swings the net back over his head, 'catching'* MRS TWIT]
[*She thrashes round inside. They sort themselves out. They advance again, nearer and nearer. Suddenly . . .*]

Charge! [*He trips over the net, which clatters to the ground*]
[*The noise frightens the* BIRDS, *who fly away and exit*]

[*The* MUGGLE-WUMPS *happily applaud.* MR TWIT *looks meaningfully at them. They stop and settle.* MRS TWIT *laughs scornfully*]

You clumsy warthog!

MRS TWIT: Clumsy yourself!

MR TWIT: It was your fault!

MRS TWIT: It wasn't my fault!

MR TWIT: It was!

MRS TWIT: It wasn't!

MR TWIT: Was!

MRS TWIT: Wasn't, wasn't, wasn't!

[*They freeze, looking furiously at each other. The* NARRATOR *steps in*]

NARRATOR: Tonight, thankfully, was not to be Bird Pie Night!

[*Curtain down*]

UPSIDE DOWN TWITS

This is the longest and most complex of the plays. It could work well as a school play, having many meaty acting roles, plus great opportunities for the art department. The play dramatizes perhaps the most memorable sequence in the book, when the Twits are fooled into believing that the world has turned upside down. It is the only play to feature audience participation—the audience help trick the Twits – which is great fun but does need clarity of direction and intention.

CHARACTERS
Narrator

Mr Twit: wearing his ill-fitting suit and, occasionally, his explorer's hat.

The Muggle-Wumps (Muggle-Wump, Mrs Muggle-Wump and their children, Muggle-Wumps 1, 2 and 3): wearing monkey costumes, plus their simple circus outfits.

Mrs Twit: wearing her long skirt and top; in the 'key' scene, an apron with a pocket could be useful.

The Birds (several puppeteers carrying birds on poles —either individual birds or a 'spray' of several birds):

the puppeteers could be dressed in jeans and T-shirts or in bird costumes.

Audience.

The Roly-Poly Bird: the actor can be male or female and should be dressed in colourful, exotic plumage; swinging on a rope to suggest flight would be effective.

Two Birds (single birds on poles carried by two puppeteers): the birds have glue brushes in their beaks.

SETTING

A central acting area, the floor of which could be painted to suggest a circus ring, is surrounded by the Big Dead Tree, the Muggle-Wumps' cage and the Twits' caravan.

The tree can be a cut-out with branches on which the Birds can perch.

The cage, with bars and a door, can also be a cut-out.

The caravan can be a cut-out painted to resemble a room inside. The furniture needs to turn upside down, which could be achieved using cut-out shapes attached with Velcro.

Behind the caravan there should be enough space for the Twits to stand, hidden from the audience.

If the stage has curtains, the opening introductory scene could be performed in front of them.

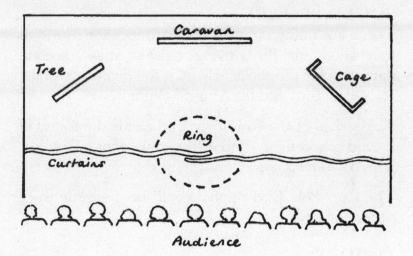

PROPS

Mrs Twit's walking stick.

Key to the cage door.

Bowl of bananas for the Muggle-Wumps.

A ladder.

A pot marked 'Hugtight Glue'.

A cooking-pot marked 'Bird Pie'.

Two shotguns: these could be cut-outs.

A puppet cut-out of the Roly-Poly Bird and the Muggle-Wumps in flight.

SOUND EFFECTS

There are many optional opportunities for music or percussion: the Birds flying, tension music, accompaniment for the spoken rhymes, the departure of the Roly-Poly Bird and the Muggle-Wumps.

The arrival of the Roly-Poly Bird needs the sound of a loud whooshing wind effect, plus wings flapping. This could be recorded.

The Roly-Poly Bird's signal could be a whistle worn round the neck.

LIGHTING

One general lighting state could suffice, but it would be effective to be able to highlight individually the tree, the cage, the caravan and the circus ring as appropriate.

An exciting effect could accompany the arrival of the Roly-Poly Bird: for example, the lighting could darken, then flash.

When the audience join in, the auditorium lights could be turned on.

A strobe or flashing light could enhance the 'turning the caravan upside down' scene, making it resemble a silent film.

UPSIDE DOWN TWITS

NARRATOR: The extremely unpleasant Mr Twit . . .
[MR TWIT *enters with a stick and poses like a big-game hunter*]

. . . goes to the rainforest of Africa and catches a family of Monkeys—the Muggle-Wumps.
[*The* MUGGLE-WUMPS *enter, animated and bright.* MR TWIT *gestures threateningly and they cower, frightened*]

He brings them back to England, where he will train them to appear in his Monkey Circus.
[MR TWIT *gestures and the* MUGGLE-WUMPS *take up a circus pose*]

The equally extremely unpleasant Mrs Twit . . .
[MRS TWIT *enters, grabs the stick and threatens* MR TWIT *with it. They freeze*]

. . . helps him lock the Muggle-Wumps . . .
[*Curtain up*]

. . . inside a cage.
[MR *and* MRS TWIT *drive the* MUGGLE-WUMPS *towards the cage and push them inside, then* MR TWIT *locks the door. He takes the key and* MR *and* MRS TWIT *exit behind the caravan. The* MUGGLE-WUMPS *relax*]

[*Indicating . . .*]

Near the cage and the Twits' caravan stood the Big Dead Tree. Every evening, as the sun went down, birds would fly in from all around to roost for the night on its branches.

[*Music as the* BIRDS *enter and fly in formation around the stage — a choreographed sequence. Then they land on the tree*]

The extremely unpleasant Twits plan to catch the birds one day and bake them in a Bird Pie. This morning, as the Muggle-Wumps wake up . . .

[*The* MUGGLE-WUMPS *yawn and stretch*]

LITTLE MUGGLE-WUMP 1: Mum! Dad!

LITTLE MUGGLE-WUMP 2: Look!

LITTLE MUGGLE-WUMP 3: The birds are still here!

NARRATOR: The birds had stayed later than usual. The night before they had been curious to see the Muggle-Wumps in their cage. They didn't like to see other creatures locked up, robbed of their freedom. They felt sorry for them.

[*The* NARRATOR *exits*]

MUGGLE-WUMP: [*Calling*] Hello, birds! Come on over!

MUGGLE-WUMPS: Come on! Come on!

[*The* BIRDS *fly over and land on the cage*]

MUGGLE-WUMP: Good morning!

[*The* BIRDS *twitter*]

LITTLE MUGGLE-WUMP 1: What are they saying, Dad?

MUGGLE-WUMP: Good morning, I suppose.

MRS MUGGLE-WUMP: We can't understand their language.
[*The* BIRDS *twitter*]

LITTLE MUGGLE-WUMP 2: Why not, Mum?

MRS MUGGLE-WUMP: They're English birds.

LITTLE MUGGLE-WUMP 3: Maybe they could help us get home.

MUGGLE-WUMP: How? They're only birds.
[*The* BIRDS *twitter*]

LITTLE MUGGLE-WUMP 1: The Roly-Poly Bird could help us.

MUGGLE-WUMP: He's in Africa.

LITTLE MUGGLE-WUMP 2: [*To the* BIRDS] Do you know the Roly-Poly Bird?

LITTLE MUGGLE-WUMP 3: He's our best friend.

MRS MUGGLE-WUMP: Of course they don't.
[*Suddenly* MR TWIT *enters with a stick from behind the caravan*]

MUGGLE-WUMP: Shhh. Look out!

MR TWIT: Come on, my lovelies. Training time!

LITTLE MUGGLE-WUMPS: Oh, no.

MUGGLE-WUMP: Shhh.

MR TWIT: [*Seeing the* BIRDS] Clear off, you pesky birds.
Don't want you messing my lovelies' cage. [*He waves*
MRS TWIT*'s stick and rattles the bars*]
   [*The* BIRDS *fly off and return to the tree. They watch
   as* MR TWIT *opens the cage door with the key. The*
   MUGGLE-WUMPS *venture out, stretching their limbs*]

Out you come. [*He contains them in the 'ring' with the
stick*] Stay! Stay! Still. Now, listen, my lovelies. I've
had a wheeze, a brilliant idea. Mr Twit's Miracu-
lous Monkey Act needs to be different. Original.
Unique. So from now on you will perform your
tricks – wait for it, it's classic – you will perform
your tricks . . . UPSIDE DOWN. The world's first
Great Upside Down Monkey Circus!
   [*The* MUGGLE-WUMPS *look on bemused, unable to
   understand*]

Look, like this, my lovelies. [*He tries to stand on his
head. He falls over. He gets up*] Well, something like
that. Right, come on, then. Up and over. Up and
over. On your hands!
   [*Circus music as the* MUGGLE-WUMPS *are forced
   into various positions. They attempt acrobatic tricks with
   varying degrees of success*]

MR TWIT: [*As appropriate*] Up! Down! Over! Stay!
Arms out! Climb! Go!

[*After several different configurations, they all attempt a kind of upside down tableau. This should be as impressive as possible*]

Hold it there. Stop wobbling! Yes! Yes! It's coming! It's coming! Well done, my lovelies. Down, down, back in the cage now. [*He allows them to stand again and forces them back into the cage*] Clever, clever. You deserve some breakfast, yes, you do. Bananas and monkey nuts, coming right up. Good monkeys. Good monkeys. [*He locks the cage door, pockets the key and starts to go back to the caravan. The music stops*]
[*The* BIRDS *twitter.* MR TWIT *sees them*]

Clear off! When we want an audience, we'll invite one. Clear off! [*He brandishes the stick*]
[*The* BIRDS *fly up and exit*]

[MR TWIT *exits happily behind the caravan*]

[*The* NARRATOR *enters*]

NARRATOR: Mr Twit was happy with his monkeys' progress. His happiness was not shared by the Muggle-Wumps.
[*In the cage the* MUGGLE-WUMPS *unwind*]

LITTLE MUGGLE-WUMP 1: I feel giddy.

LITTLE MUGGLE-WUMP 2: I feel dizzy.

LITTLE MUGGLE-WUMP 3: I feel sick.

MRS MUGGLE-WUMP: Take deep breaths, children.

[*To her husband*] Oh, Muggle-Wump, why does that horrid man make us do such stupid, undignified things?

MUGGLE-WUMP: I don't know, dear, but I do know that if we stay here much longer, the children will grow ill. They may even die.

MRS MUGGLE-WUMP: Die?

LITTLE MUGGLE-WUMPS: [*Overhearing*] Die?

MRS MUGGLE-WUMP: No, no, children. [*She thinks quickly*] Try.

MUGGLE-WUMP: Yes, try. We must all try to be brave, like the Roly-Poly Bird said when we . . .

MRS MUGGLE-WUMP: . . . when he said goodbye. Try to be brave. Yes?

LITTLE MUGGLE-WUMPS: We'll try. [*But they begin to sob*]

MUGGLE-WUMP: [*Frustrated*] We've got to get out of this cage. [*He rattles the bars*]

MRS MUGGLE-WUMP: But how?

MUGGLE-WUMP: [*Having an idea*] The door! The man opens it with a special thing. He puts it in, turns it and the door opens.

MRS MUGGLE-WUMP: What's it called? [*To the* AUDIENCE] Does anyone know?

AUDIENCE: Key!

MUGGLE-WUMP: A what?

AUDIENCE: Key!

MRS MUGGLE-WUMP: Thank you!

MUGGLE-WUMP: The key. [*Excitedly, to his family*] We'll steal the key.

MRS MUGGLE-WUMP: But how?

MUGGLE-WUMP: I don't know yet, but . . .

MRS MUGGLE-WUMP: [*Having an idea, to the* AUDIENCE] Will *you* help us?

AUDIENCE: Yes!

MUGGLE-WUMP: You will?

AUDIENCE: Yes!

MUGGLE-WUMP: Thank you. Now, when . . .
    [MR *and* MRS TWIT *enter from behind the caravan.* MRS TWIT *carries the bowl of bananas*]

NARRATOR: Look out, Muggle-Wumps!

MRS MUGGLE-WUMP: Shh! They're coming!
    [*The* MUGGLE-WUMPS *settle. The* NARRATOR *exits*]

MR TWIT: Don't forget. They're only allowed to eat upside down.

MRS TWIT: All right, all right. Where's the key?

[MR TWIT *hands* MRS TWIT *the key, then starts to return behind the caravan*]

MR TWIT: [*Turning*] Upside down!

MRS TWIT: I know. Keep your hair on!
[MR TWIT *exits*]

[MRS TWIT *puts the key in the lock*]

Right, come on, you ugly lot. Upside down or no breakfast. [*She opens the cage door, leaving the key in the lock, then enters the cage to put down the bowl of bananas*] Up on your hands! Move! [*She prods them with her stick*]
[*Unseen by* MRS TWIT, MUGGLE-WUMP *slips out of the cage and deftly removes the key from the lock*]

MUGGLE-WUMP: [*Whispering to the* AUDIENCE] I've got it! [*He nips back inside*]

MRS TWIT: Upside down, I said!
[*All the* MUGGLE-WUMPS *manage to stand or crouch upside down*]

That's better. Now, eat. [*She emerges and closes the door*]
[*Before she has time to think about locking it,* MR TWIT *appears and shouts from the caravan*]

MR TWIT: Are they upside down?

MRS TWIT: [*Moving towards* MR TWIT] Yes, yes.

MR TWIT: All of them? Little ones too?

MRS TWIT: Little ones too. See for yourself.
[MR TWIT *goes to the cage and looks*]

MR TWIT: [*Triumphantly*] Yes! Yes! [*He returns behind the caravan, passing* MRS TWIT]
[MRS TWIT *returns to the cage. She reaches for the key, but it's not in the lock*]

MRS TWIT: Funny. [*To herself*] Where's the key? [*She delves into a pocket*] Not there.
[*She thinks. Then she tries to pull the door open.* MUGGLE-WUMP *is holding it shut from inside*]

Mmm. It's locked all right. I must have locked it. [*To herself*] Then where's the key? [*She checks her pocket again, then notices the* AUDIENCE] 'Ere, you lot, did I lock that door?
[*If necessary, the* MUGGLE-WUMPS *encourage the* AUDIENCE *to fool* MRS TWIT]

AUDIENCE: Yes.

MRS TWIT: Are you sure?

AUDIENCE: Yes.

MRS TWIT: Did Mr Twit take the key?

AUDIENCE: Yes.

MRS TWIT: Are you sure?

AUDIENCE: Yes.

MRS TWIT: Oh. [*Suspiciously*] You're not having me on, are you?

AUDIENCE: No.

MRS TWIT: Cos if you are, you'll feel my big stick on your little bums, d'you hear? [*She brandishes her stick and probably gets booed as a result. She then exits behind the caravan*]
[*In the cage,* MUGGLE-WUMP *holds up the key*]

MUGGLE-WUMP: [*To the* AUDIENCE] Thank you! [*To the other* MUGGLE-WUMPS] I've got it! [*He holds up the key*] We fooled her!
[*Cheers. The* MUGGLE-WUMPS *jump up and down with excitement*]

Come on, Muggle-Wumps! We're going home! [*Carefully, he starts to open the cage door and leads the others out*]

[*But suddenly* MR TWIT *enters from behind the caravan, carrying a ladder*]

[*The* AUDIENCE *possibly shout a warning. In any event . . .*]

Aaaaah! Back in! Back in!
[*The* MUGGLE-WUMPS *scramble back and turn upside down.* MUGGLE-WUMP *closes the cage door.* MR TWIT *takes a quick look at the* MUGGLE-WUMPS *to check they are upside down, then heads for the tree. As he leans the ladder against the tree, the* NARRATOR *enters*]

NARRATOR: Mr Twit now turned his evil attention towards . . . the birds.

[MR TWIT *returns briefly behind the caravan*]

His twisted, nasty, cruel mind had come up with another twisted, nasty, cruel idea.

[MR TWIT *comes back carrying a large pot marked 'Hugtight Glue'. He climbs the ladder and, using a large paintbrush, coats the top of the branches of the tree with the glue*]

MR TWIT: [*As he works*]
Coat ev'ry branch with Hugtight Glue,
Birds, I've a big surprise for you!
Slop it and slap it and spread it along,
Soon you'll sing your final song!
Land on the tree
And you'll never get free!
Tough titties, hard luck,
You'll be stuck, stuck, stuck!
So stand by, birds, for a great big fright,
Stand by, Twits, it's Bird Pie night!

[*Laughing cruelly,* MR TWIT *climbs down and carries the ladder and the pot of glue back behind the caravan*]

[MUGGLE-WUMP *opens the cage door and the* MUGGLE-WUMPS *all creep softly out, holding hands*]

MUGGLE-WUMP: Come on! We're free! We're free!

[*As they reach the centre of the 'ring' they are stopped in their tracks by a terrifying sound, a gale-force wind accompanied by a loud flapping noise. The* MUGGLE-WUMPS *start to panic. Exciting lighting effects could heighten the drama*]

MRS MUGGLE-WUMP: What's happening?

LITTLE MUGGLE-WUMPS: Help! Help!

MUGGLE-WUMP: It must be a storm!
[*The* MUGGLE-WUMPS, *arms flailing, dash to and fro, bumping into each other. As the sound effects intensify, they all look to* MUGGLE-WUMP *for guidance*]

[*Shouting . . .*]

Take shelter in the tree!

MRS MUGGLE-WUMP: [*Shouting*] In the tree? Are you sure?

MUGGLE-WUMP: [*Shouting*] We'll be safe there! To . . . the . . . tree!
[MRS MUGGLE-WUMP *nods her agreement*]

MUGGLE-WUMP and MRS MUGGLE-WUMP: [*Together, to the* LITTLE MUGGLE-WUMPS] Climb the tree!
[*In slow motion, the* MUGGLE-WUMPS *head for the tree. Hopefully, the* AUDIENCE, *knowing the tree is coated with glue, shout out a warning. The tension and audience participation build towards a climax as the* MUGGLE-WUMPS *get nearer and nearer the tree*]

[*Suddenly the lighting and sound effects stop. The* LITTLE MUGGLE-WUMPS *look up and point to the sky*]

LITTLE MUGGLE-WUMP 1: Mum!

LITTLE MUGGLE-WUMP 2: Dad!

LITTLE MUGGLE-WUMP 3: Look!

ALL MUGGLE-WUMPS: [*Looking up*] It's the Roly-Poly Bird!

MUGGLE-WUMP: It wasn't a storm. It was the Roly-Poly Bird!
[*The* ROLY-POLY BIRD *'flies' joyfully in. The* MUGGLE-WUMPS *cheer*]

ROLY-POLY BIRD: Hello, Muggle-Wump! Hello, Mrs Muggle-Wump! Hello, little Muggle-Wumps!

MUGGLE-WUMPS: Hello, Roly-Poly Bird!

MUGGLE-WUMP: You've come!

ROLY-POLY BIRD: Of course. I promised I would! And the Roly-Poly Bird never breaks a promise. I promised I would come!

MRS MUGGLE-WUMP: But not till the spring.

ROLY-POLY BIRD: I was worried about you. I came early.

MRS MUGGLE-WUMP: Thank you.

ROLY-POLY BIRD: Have you been brave? Are your tails up? Are your heads held high?

MUGGLE-WUMP: Of course.

MRS MUGGLE-WUMP: We're free!

ROLY-POLY BIRD: Why are you dressed in those silly, degrading clothes?

MUGGLE-WUMP: They made us.

ROLY-POLY BIRD: They? Who are they? [*He sees the* AUDIENCE, *with a gasp*] Them?

MUGGLE-WUMP: No, no. These are our friends. They helped us escape.

ROLY-POLY BIRD: Escape?

MRS MUGGLE-WUMP: From that cage. They locked us in.

ROLY-POLY BIRD: [*Indicating the* AUDIENCE] *They* did?

MUGGLE-WUMP: No!

ROLY-POLY BIRD: [*To the* AUDIENCE] Then *who* did?

AUDIENCE: The Twits!

ROLY-POLY BIRD: Who?

AUDIENCE: The Twits!

ROLY-POLY BIRD: The Twits?

MUGGLE-WUMP: Yes. They made us perform tricks.

LITTLE MUGGLE-WUMPS: Upside down!

ROLY-POLY BIRD: Upside down! Unnatural! Outrageous! These Twits must be taught a lesson. [*To the* AUDIENCE] Mustn't they?

AUDIENCE: Yes!

MUGGLE-WUMP: But we can't stay here.

MRS MUGGLE-WUMP: The Twits might catch us again.

ROLY-POLY BIRD: I see. Let me think, let me think, let me think! [*He has an idea*] Ah! Inspiration! Quick, Muggle-Wumps, climb up that tree. We can plan in safety there.
   [*The* MUGGLE-WUMPS *and the* ROLY-POLY BIRD *head for the tree. The* AUDIENCE *react*]

AUDIENCE: No!
   [*The* MUGGLE-WUMPS *and the* ROLY-POLY BIRD *stop*]

ROLY-POLY BIRD: [*To the* AUDIENCE] Why not?

AUDIENCE: There's glue on the tree!

ROLY-POLY BIRD: Glue? [*He carefully moves to the tree. He looks and sniffs. To the* MUGGLE-WUMPS] Your friends are right. Glue.

MUGGLE-WUMP: What's glue?

ROLY-POLY BIRD: Horrid sticky stuff. [*To the* AUDIENCE] Who put it there?

AUDIENCE: The Twits.

ROLY-POLY BIRD: Why?

AUDIENCE: To catch the birds.

ROLY-POLY BIRD: [*Horrified*] To catch the birds!

MUGGLE-WUMP: We know them. They often perch there.

ROLY-POLY BIRD: [*To the* AUDIENCE] But why should the Twits want to catch them?

AUDIENCE: To eat them . . . To make a Bird Pie.

ROLY-POLY BIRD: [*Even more horrified*] To eat them in a Bird Pie?

AUDIENCE: Yes.

ROLY-POLY BIRD: Barbarous! Brutal! Beastly!

MUGGLE-WUMP: The birds may fly back soon.

MRS MUGGLE-WUMP: We must warn them!

ROLY-POLY BIRD: Indeed we must.

MUGGLE-WUMP: But they don't understand us!

ROLY-POLY BIRD: They'll understand me! I'm a bird too. [*He takes in the* AUDIENCE] And our friends will help. Won't you?

AUDIENCE: Yes.
    [*The* MUGGLE-WUMPS *react happily*]

ROLY-POLY BIRD: Excellent. Now, let me think, let me think, let me think. [*Suddenly*] Ah! Inspiration!
When the birds are very near
Near enough for them to hear
We'll shout this rhyme – loud and clear . . .
[*Pause, as the* ROLY-POLY BIRD *concentrates*]

There's sticky stick stuff all over the tree!
If you land in the branches, you'll never get free!
So fly away! Fly away! Stay up high!
Or you'll finish up tonight in a hot Bird Pie!

Got it? Now, everybody . . .

There's sticky stick stuff all over . . .
[*He meanders to a halt, because the participation is limited*]

Where were you? Where were you?

MUGGLE-WUMP: We need to learn it first, Roly-Poly Bird.

ROLY-POLY BIRD: Of course! After me . . .
There's sticky stick stuff all over the tree!
[*The* AUDIENCE *join in with them all*]

ALL: There's sticky stick stuff all over the tree!

ROLY-POLY BIRD: If you land in the branches, you'll never get free!

ALL: If you land in the branches, you'll never get free!

ROLY-POLY BIRD: So fly away! Fly away! Stay up high!

ALL: So fly away! Fly away! Stay up high!

ROLY-POLY BIRD: Or you'll finish up tonight in a hot Bird Pie!

ALL: Or you'll finish up tonight in a hot Bird Pie!

ROLY-POLY BIRD: Good! Let's put it all together. And listen, to make sure we all say it at the same time, I'll give a signal. [*He thinks*] How about this? [*He makes a loud piercing whistle*] Yes? Ready, then. Good and loud! Wait for the signal. [*He whistles*]

ALL: There's sticky stick stuff all over the tree!
If you land in the branches, you'll never get free!
So fly away! Fly away! Stay up high!
Or you'll finish up tonight in a hot Bird Pie!

ROLY-POLY BIRD: Excellent. Thank you!
[*The* MUGGLE-WUMPS *cheer and jump about with excitement. Suddenly they hear a loud voice*]

MR TWIT: [*Off, loudly*] Hurry up! Get a move on!
[*There is an instant change of mood. The* MUGGLE-WUMPS *tremble and dither*]

LITTLE MUGGLE-WUMP 1: [*Quickly*] Mum!

LITTLE MUGGLE-WUMP 2: [*Quickly*] Dad!

LITTLE MUGGLE-WUMP 3: It's them!

MUGGLE-WUMP and MRS MUGGLE-WUMP: [*Together*] The Twits!

ROLY-POLY BIRD: [*Taking control*] Quick! Back in the cage!
  [*The* MUGGLE-WUMPS *hurry back inside the cage, closing the door, then stand or crouch upside down. The* ROLY-POLY BIRD *positions himself out of sight of the* TWITS, *but in view of the* AUDIENCE. *Ideally he should be above the action; perhaps he could climb on the cage*]

  [MR TWIT *enters from behind the caravan*]

MR TWIT: [*Shouting*] Come on, you dozy doughnut, shift yourself!
  [MRS TWIT *enters with a large cooking pot marked 'Bird Pie'*]

MRS TWIT: Pipe down, you hairy great turnip. I'm behind you.

MR TWIT: You don't want to miss all the fun.

MRS TWIT: So long as it works. [*She sees the* MUGGLE-WUMPS *and prods through the cage bars with her walking stick*] Get up! Get up!
  [*The* MUGGLE-WUMPS *shuffle about*]

MR TWIT: Of course it'll work. Can't fail. We'll stand over here and watch.
  [*The* TWITS *position themselves to one side*]

So stand by, birds, for a great big fright.

MR and MRS TWIT: [*Together*] Stand by, Twits, it's Bird Pie night! [*They cackle in evil anticipation*]

MR TWIT: [*Pointing up*] They're coming! They're coming!

MRS TWIT: Shhhh.
[*They watch*]

[*The* BIRDS *enter. They fly around for a circuit or two. Then they hover above the tree. The* ROLY-POLY BIRD *whistles*]

ALL EXCEPT THE TWITS:
There's sticky stick stuff all over the tree!
If you land in the branches, you'll never get free!
So fly away! Fly away! Stay up high!
Or you'll finish up tonight in a hot Bird Pie!
[*The* BIRDS *retreat. They fly up and away from the tree and land safely on the cage. The* TWITS *emerge. The* ROLY-POLY BIRD, *the* MUGGLE-WUMPS *and the* AUDIENCE *cheer*]

MR TWIT: No! Over there! You're meant to be on the tree over there!
[*The* BIRDS *twitter, bobbing cockily up and down on the cage*]

MRS TWIT: Typical! You silly, great twit, you're useless! [*She storms back behind the caravan with her Bird Pie pot*]

MR TWIT: [*Furious in defeat*] Oooooh! It's not fair!
[*The* BIRDS *twitter, the* MUGGLE-WUMPS *chatter.
Hopefully the* AUDIENCE *laugh*]

It's not funny! [*To the* MUGGLE-WUMPS] Shut up! [*To
the* AUDIENCE] Shut up!
[*Eventually* . . .]

Right, that's it! [*He scares off the* BIRDS *with a huge
gesture*]
[*The* BIRDS *fly away and exit*]

[MR TWIT *dashes back behind the caravan*]

[*The* NARRATOR *enters*]

NARRATOR: Mr Twit was not a man to be laughed at.
He was not a man to be easily beaten.
[MR TWIT *enters with the ladder and the glue pot. He
leans the ladder against the cage*]

Bird Pie he wanted. And Bird Pie he was determined
to have.

[*The* NARRATOR *exits*]

[MR TWIT *climbs the ladder and paints the top of the
cage with glue. The* MUGGLE-WUMPS *cower below, not
wanting to be splattered with glue*]

MR TWIT: [*Challengingly*] Now I'll get you! Which-
ever one you sit on! [*He cackles, climbs down, collects the
ladder and exits behind the caravan*]

ROLY-POLY BIRD: All clear!
[*The* MUGGLE-WUMPS *come out of the cage, stretching their limbs. The* ROLY-POLY BIRD *'flies' down to meet them*]

MUGGLE-WUMP: [*To the* AUDIENCE] Thank you, everyone, you saved the birds!

ROLY-POLY BIRD: But not for long, Muggle-Wump. We must warn them again. Let me think, let me think, let me think! [*He pauses for thought*] Ah! Inspiration! After me, everyone . . . There's sticky stuff now on the cage *and* the tree!

ALL: There's sticky stuff now on the cage *and* the tree!

ROLY-POLY BIRD: If you land on the cage, you'll never get free!

ALL: If you land on the cage, you'll never get free!

ROLY-POLY BIRD: So fly away! Fly away! Stay up high!

ALL: So fly away! Fly away! Stay up high!

ROLY-POLY BIRD: Or you'll finish up tonight in a hot Bird Pie!

ALL: Or you'll finish up tonight in a hot Bird Pie!

ROLY-POLY BIRD: Excellent! Let's put it all together. After the signal. [*He whistles*]

ALL: There's sticky stuff now on the cage *and* the tree!
If you land on the cage, you'll never get free!
So fly away! Fly away! Stay up high!
Or you'll finish up tonight in a hot Bird Pie!

ROLY-POLY BIRD: Thank you. Good luck!

MR TWIT: [*Off*] Come on!

MUGGLE-WUMP: Quick!
[*The* MUGGLE-WUMPS *hurry back into the cage and stand or crouch upside down. The* ROLY-POLY BIRD *moves away*]

[MR *and* MRS TWIT *enter, carrying the Bird Pie pot*]

MRS TWIT: [*Doubtfully*] Here we go again.

MR TWIT: This time, my luscious little humbug, we cannot fail!
[*They position themselves to one side*]

Stand by, birds, for a great big fright.

MR and MRS TWIT: [*Together*] Stand by, Twits, it's Bird Pie night!
[*The* BIRDS *enter. They circle, then hover above the tree, then swoop up and over the cage*]

[*The* ROLY-POLY BIRD *whistles*]

ALL EXCEPT THE TWITS:
There's sticky stuff now on the cage *and* the tree!
If you land on the cage, you'll never get free!
So fly away! Fly away! Stay up high!
Or you'll finish up tonight in a hot Bird Pie!

[*The* BIRDS *react. They fly up and away from the cage. They go over to the caravan and land safely on the roof*]

MR TWIT: No! No! Aaaaah! It's not fair!
[*The* BIRDS *twitter, the* MUGGLE-WUMPS *chatter, the* AUDIENCE *hopefully laugh*]

It's not funny!
[*More laughter*]

MRS TWIT: It's not funny. It's pathetic. Bird Pie? No chance.

MR TWIT: [*Suddenly realizing, noticing the* AUDIENCE] It was them!

MRS TWIT: What?

MR TWIT: Warning the birds. It was *them*. [*To the* AUDIENCE] You smarmy little goody-goodies!

MRS TWIT: [*To the* AUDIENCE] You sneaky little sissies!

MR TWIT: You squealing little blabbers, you blabbing little squealers!

MRS TWIT: You'll pay for that!

MR TWIT: Through the toes!

MRS TWIT: Nose!

MR TWIT: [*Thinking* MRS TWIT *said 'No'*] Yes!

MRS TWIT: Nose!

MR TWIT: Yes!

MRS TWIT: Oh, never mind.

MR TWIT: [*To the* AUDIENCE] If you make one squeak next time, I'll glue you to your seats!

MRS TWIT: Next time? What do you mean, next time?

MR TWIT: Third time lucky? [*He remembers the* BIRDS *are on the roof and therefore talks in a loud whisper*] I'll glue the roof!

MRS TWIT: [*Also speaking in a loud whisper*] Roof? What roof?

MR TWIT: The roof of the caravan.

MRS TWIT: [*Shouting*] Over my dead body!

MR TWIT: Shhh.

MRS TWIT: [*In a loud whisper*] Over my dead body. I'm not having you smearing sticky glue all over the roof of our caravan. [*She threatens him with her stick*]

MR TWIT: [*A frustrated shout of rage*] Ooooooh! [*He runs towards the caravan, shaking his fists at the* BIRDS]
[*The* BIRDS *fly up a little, then back on to the roof, twittering*]

I'll wipe that silly laugh off your beaks! I'll get you, you feathery frumps! I'll wring your necks, the whole lot of you. I'll have you bubbling in the Bird Pie pot before this day is out!

MRS TWIT: Huh! Promises, promises.
[MR TWIT *strives to think of an idea. Suddenly . . .*]

MR TWIT: I've got it! A great idea. We'll both go into town right away and we'll each buy . . . a gun! How's that?

MRS TWIT: Brilliant! We'll buy those big shotguns that spray out fifty bullets or more with each bang!

MR TWIT: Perfect!
[*He notices the* MUGGLE-WUMPS, *who are no longer upside down, but standing watching.* MR TWIT *approaches the cage*]

And you lot. Upside down and jump to it!

MRS TWIT: [*Joining him*] Quick! Get on with it or you'll feel my stick!
[*The* MUGGLE-WUMPS *struggle back into upside down positions*]

MR TWIT: Now stay there till we come back.
[MR *and* MRS TWIT *exit*]

[*After a pause, the* ROLY-POLY BIRD *checks that the* TWITS *have gone*]

ROLY-POLY BIRD: All clear!
[*The* MUGGLE-WUMPS *stand upright and come out of the cage*]

[*The* NARRATOR *enters*]

NARRATOR: With the Twits out of the way for a while, the Roly-Poly Bird announced . . .

ROLY-POLY BIRD: It is time for a conference!

LITTLE MUGGLE-WUMP I: What's a conference?

MUGGLE-WUMP: A meeting.

NARRATOR: Everyone was invited. The Muggle-Wumps!
[*The* MUGGLE-WUMPS *gather*]

The birds!
[*Music as the* BIRDS *fly from the roof and hover above the 'ring'*]

And the Roly-Poly Bird himself!
[*The* ROLY-POLY BIRD *'takes the chair'*]

Many subjects were discussed.
[*All animatedly mime discussion. Then . . .*]

ROLY-POLY BIRD: Freedom for Muggle-Wumps!

MUGGLE-WUMP: Protection for the birds!

MRS MUGGLE-WUMP and LITTLE MUGGLE-WUMPS:
[*Together*] Down with the Twits!
[*The* BIRDS *do a twittering echo of 'Down with the Twits'. The mimed discussion continues*]

NARRATOR: It was agreed that . . .

ALL: Down with the Twits!

NARRATOR: . . . should be their first target. If the Twits could be defeated, the Muggle-Wumps would be free and the birds would be safe.

ALL: Down with the Twits!

ROLY-POLY BIRD: But how?
[*More animated mimed 'discussion'. Then . . .*]

MUGGLE-WUMP: Teach them a lesson!

MRS MUGGLE-WUMP: Lock them in the cage!

ROLY-POLY BIRD: Glue them to the roof!

BIRD OPERATOR 1: Peck their noses!

BIRD OPERATOR 2: Make Twit Pie!

BIRD OPERATOR 3: Give them a bath!

LITTLE MUGGLE-WUMP 1: Prod them with a stick!

LITTLE MUGGLE-WUMP 2: Make them do tricks!

LITTLE MUGGLE-WUMP 3: Turn them upside down!
[*A pause. A gasp*]

ROLY-POLY BIRD: What was that?

LITTLE MUGGLE-WUMP 3: Turn them upside down!
[*All react in a delighted fashion*]

ALL: Turn them upside down!

NARRATOR: Everyone set to work!
[*Exciting music. A flurry of activity. The idea of the*

sequence is that all the animals and birds make the caravan interior look upside down by gluing the carpet and the furniture to the ceiling. The ROLY-POLY BIRD *supervises operations. The* MUGGLE-WUMPS, *led by* MUGGLE-WUMP, *find the glue pot and paintbrush and glue everything upside down. The* BIRDS *fly about above and behind the caravan. Cardboard cut-outs can be used for the furniture and, perhaps, the caravan wheels. Velcro could be used to attach things]*

[The following accompanying narration by the NARRATOR *is optional]*

The Muggle-Wumps found Mr Twit's pot of glue and lots of paintbrushes. Then everyone smeared and slapped the sticky glue all over the Twits' ceiling. The birds joined in—buzzards, magpies, rooks, ravens and many more. Then, in one mighty pull, they dragged the carpet from under the furniture and hoisted it up on to the ceiling. And there it stuck! Next, the table and chairs, the sofa, the sideboard, the lamps, the ornaments—*everything* was turned upside down, glue brushed on the bottom and then stuck on the carpeted ceiling. And finally the pictures on the wall were upturned too. Now the Twits' room was completely and utterly *upside down!*

[After the choreographed sequence and, if used, the optional narration, the final revelation is made. Everybody cheers. The NARRATOR *exits. The* ROLY-POLY BIRD *surveys the scene]*

ROLY-POLY BIRD: Expertly done! Congratulations, one and all!

MUGGLE-WUMP: The Twits will think they're upside down, the maggoty old monsters!

ROLY-POLY BIRD: But wait. Their room is upside down, you Muggle-Wumps will be upside down. But what about the birds?
   [*The* BIRDS *fly up, turn over, then land and lie on the roof upside down. The* MUGGLE-WUMPS *clap and cheer*]

MUGGLE-WUMP: Yes! [*A sudden realization*] But what about [*He indicates the* AUDIENCE] our friends?

MRS MUGGLE-WUMP: *They're* not upside down.
   [*All look concerned*]

ROLY-POLY BIRD: Let me think, let me think. Let me think! [*He pauses for thought*] Ah! Inspiration! [*To the* AUDIENCE] Everybody, please help fool the Twits. Take off your shoes! Yes, quickly, please. Take off your shoes.
   [*The* AUDIENCE *are encouraged further, if necessary, to remove their shoes*]

Now put your shoes on your hands. And stretch your arms up above your heads!
   [*The* MUGGLE-WUMPS *mime a demonstration*]

Yes, yes! Now, hold them still and lower your heads a little! Yes, yes!

MUGGLE-WUMP: You look upside down!

MRS MUGGLE-WUMP: You really do!
[*Suddenly . . .*]

MR and MRS TWIT: [*Offstage, together*] Stand by, birds, for a great big fright . . .

LITTLE MUGGLE-WUMPS: They're coming! They're coming!
[*The* MUGGLE-WUMPS *dash back to the cage and position themselves*]

ROLY-POLY BIRD: [*To the* AUDIENCE] Arms down, everyone, but shoes on hands ready. Wait for my signal! [*He hides to one side*]
[MR *and* MRS TWIT *enter, carrying big shotguns*]

MR and MRS TWIT: [*Together*] Stand by, Twits, it's Bird Pie night!
[*They reach the cage*]

MR TWIT: I'm glad to see those monkeys are still upside down.

MRS TWIT: They're too stupid to do anything else. Hey, look, those cheeky birds are still on the roof.

MR TWIT: Let's blast them with our lovely new guns!
[*They start to aim*]

MRS TWIT: Hang on! Why aren't they moving?

MR TWIT: Are they dead already?
[*The* BIRDS *flutter, rise a little, still upside down, then drop to the roof*]

MR and MRS TWIT: [*Together*] Aah! They're not dead ... they're upside down! They can't be. They *are*!
[*They stand, bemused*]

[*Two* BIRDS *enter, carrying glue brushes in their beaks. They swoop down and one brushes the top of* MR TWIT'*s head and the other the top of* MRS TWIT'*s head*]

MR and MRS TWIT: [*Together*] What was that?
[*They look up to see the* BIRDS *swoop up and fly off*]

MRS TWIT: Ugh! That beastly bird has dropped his dirty droppings on my head!

MR TWIT: On mine too! I felt it. I felt it! Ugh!

MRS TWIT: Don't touch it! You'll get it all over your hands! Come inside and we'll wash it off.

MR TWIT: [*Looking up*] Filthy, dirty brutes! I'll bet they did it on purpose. [*He brandishes his shotgun*] Just you wait! Grrrrh!
[*The* TWITS *go to the caravan. They see the upside down room. They stop and stand aghast*]

MRS TWIT: [*Gasping*] What's this?

MR TWIT: What's happened?

MRS TWIT: Look? That's the floor! The floor's up there! This is the ceiling! We're standing on the ceiling!

MR TWIT: We're upside down! We *must* be upside down. We're standing on the ceiling looking down at the floor!

MRS TWIT: Help! Help! I'm beginning to feel giddy! [*She totters*]

MR TWIT: [*Trying to convince himself*] Wait. We *can't* be upside down.

MRS TWIT: We are! We are!

MR TWIT: If *we're* upside down, the monkeys would have looked the right way up. But they didn't.

MRS TWIT: Let's look again.
[*As they return towards the cage, the* MUGGLE-WUMPS *all reverse themselves, standing upright. The* TWITS *arrive*]

MR and MRS TWIT: [*Together*] Aaaah! They're the right way up!

MR TWIT: It can't be true!

MRS TWIT: It *is* true!

MR TWIT: What about [*Indicating the* AUDIENCE, *but not looking at them*] those smarmy little goody-goodies?

MRS TWIT: What about them?

MR TWIT: They're the right way up. But if we're upside down, *they'd* look upside down.

MRS TWIT: [*Confused*] Er . . . yes.

MR TWIT: Let's have a look.
[*As they turn to move towards the* AUDIENCE, *the* ROLY-POLY BIRD *whistles. The* AUDIENCE *hold up their arms, with their shoes on their hands. The* TWITS *arrive and see the* AUDIENCE *at the same time*]

MR and MRS TWIT: [*Together*] Aaah! They're upside down!

MR TWIT: It can't be true!

MRS TWIT: It *is* true!

MR and MRS TWIT: [*Together*] Aaaaaaaaaah!
[*They stagger back to the caravan. The* ROLY-POLY BIRD *emerges*]

ROLY-POLY BIRD: [*To the* AUDIENCE] Thank you! It worked! Arms down!
[*The* AUDIENCE *drop their arms. The* ROLY-POLY BIRD *hides again. The* TWITS *arrive in their upside down room*]

MRS TWIT: [*In a panic*] We're upside down and all the blood's going to my head! If we don't do something quickly, I shall die, I know I will!

MR TWIT: I've got it! We'll stand on our heads, then we'll be the right way up again!
[MR *and* MRS TWIT *stand on their heads. The* MUGGLE-WUMPS *creep out of the cage to watch.*

The BIRDS *fly up, right themselves and swoop down to watch. The* ROLY-POLY BIRD *goes nearer too. The* NARRATOR *enters*]

NARRATOR: When the tops of their heads touched the floor, the sticky glue that the birds had brushed on a few moments before did its job. The Twits were pinned down, cemented, glued, fixed to the floorboards.

[*The* TWITS *strive unsuccessfully to get up*]

The Twits were well and truly stuck!

[*Hopefully the* AUDIENCE *cheer, along with the* MUGGLE-WUMPS, *the* ROLY-POLY BIRD *and the* BIRDS]

The birds were safe! The Muggle-Wumps were free!
[*Cheers*]

[*The* MUGGLE-WUMPS *remove their circus costumes and throw them in the cage*]

MUGGLE-WUMP: Thank you, Roly-Poly Bird.

ROLY-POLY BIRD: Everybody helped. [*He indicates the* AUDIENCE]

MUGGLE-WUMPS: [*To the* AUDIENCE] Thank you!

LITTLE MUGGLE-WUMP 1: Mum!

LITTLE MUGGLE-WUMP 2: Dad!

LITTLE MUGGLE-WUMP 3: Can we go home now?

MRS MUGGLE-WUMP: Can we go home, Roly-Poly Bird?

ROLY-POLY BIRD: You most certainly can! I shall be proud to personally escort you! Goodbye, birds!

MUGGLE-WUMPS: Goodbye, birds!
 [*The* BIRDS *twitter*]

Come, Muggle-Wumps!

MRS MUGGLE-WUMP: Hold on tight!
 [*The* MUGGLE-WUMPS *all hold hands.* MUGGLE-WUMP *holds on to the* ROLY-POLY BIRD, *who prepares for take-off*]

 [*Drum roll as the* ROLY-POLY BIRD *and the* MUGGLE-WUMPS *exit, watched by the* BIRDS]

 [*Then, as the* NARRATOR *enters and speaks, a puppeteer carries a puppet/cut-out of the* ROLY-POLY BIRD *and the* MUGGLE-WUMPS *across the stage and exits*]

NARRATOR: The Roly-Poly Bird carried the Muggle-Wumps home to the rainforest of Africa, where they could be free for evermore. The Birds flew off to find another, more friendly tree. They were free too.
 [*The* BIRDS *swoop round happily and exit*]

As for the Twits . . . [*the* NARRATOR *looks round at them*] . . . they were not free. Their world had turned well and truly upside down. And everyone shouted . . .

[*The whole* CAST *rush on stage*]

ALL: Hooray!

[*Curtain down*]

THE DREADED SHRINKS

This very short play offers the Twits a somewhat less final and deservedly bleak fate than in the original story. Instead of them disappearing completely, it leaves them alive and still arguing! It makes use of an earlier episode in the book.

CHARACTERS
Narrator

Mr Twit: wearing his ill-fitting suit and a bald wig.

Mrs Twit: wearing her long skirt and top and a bald wig.

The Birds: two or three puppeteers carrying birds on poles with pins attached to their beaks.

SETTING
An empty space.

Ideally Mrs Twit should 'fly', but this would involve a complicated harness and specially rigged flying wire. Her ascent can be satisfactorily mimed using the different levels of a table and chair, or a set of rostrum steps.

PROPS
Two or three bunches of helium balloons.
Two wigs 'glued' to the floor.
Mrs Twit's walking stick.

SOUND EFFECTS
No special effects are required, but percussion sounds
to accompany Mrs Twit's 'flight' could be fun.

LIGHTING
A follow spot on Mrs Twit's upper half as she ascends
might help the illusion of flight.

THE DREADED SHRINKS

NARRATOR: The disgusting Mr and Mrs Twit enjoy playing nasty tricks on each other and everybody else. But now they have had their come-uppance. The Muggle-Wump family and the Birds, led by the clever Roly-Poly Bird, have fooled them into thinking that their world has turned upside down. They are so stupid that they have tried to solve the problem by standing on their heads, little realizing that they have become firmly stuck to the floor with Hugtight Glue.

[*Curtain up, revealing the* TWITS *standing on their heads*]

After a few deservedly uncomfortable days, the Twits managed to struggle free.

[*The* TWITS *struggle, fall over, then stand up. They are bald. Their hair remains glued to the floor.* MRS TWIT *is hunched up and stooping. She picks up her walking stick*]

Soon even they realized it was the room that was upside down, not them. They blamed each other for their stupid mistake, but never found out who had played such a clever trick on them. They were furious that the Monkeys had escaped.

THE TWITS: Aaaaaah!

NARRATOR: And that Bird Pie would never be on the menu.

THE TWITS: Aaaaaah!

NARRATOR: Now they had nothing left to do but the one thing they were best at – being nasty to each other.

MR TWIT: You look all squashed down, my hunchy dumpling.

MRS TWIT: I *feel* all squashed down, you whiskery old walrus. It's your fault. You said to stand on our heads!

MR TWIT: I reckon as you're developing 'the dreaded shrinks'.

MRS TWIT: No! Not 'the dreaded shrinks'!

MR TWIT: I reckon. Your head shrinks into your body. Then your body shrinks into your legs. Then your legs shrink into your feet. Then there's nothing left except a pair of old shoes and a bundle of old clothes.

MRS TWIT: I can't bear it!

MR TWIT: It's a terrible disease. The worst in the world.

MRS TWIT: But isn't there anything we can do?

MR TWIT: There's only one cure for 'the dreaded shrinks'.

MRS TWIT: Tell me!

MR TWIT: You must be stretched!
[MR TWIT *fetches several bunches of helium balloons. He attaches them to* MRS TWIT. *As more and more balloons are added, her body starts to straighten up*]

Can you feel the balloons stretching you?

MRS TWIT: I can! I can!
[*A few more balloons are added.* MRS TWIT *starts to rise up in the air. She climbs on a chair.* MR TWIT *holds on to her ankles*]

Aaaaah! Ooooooh!
[MR TWIT *looks pleased with himself*]

You are holding on to me, aren't you? If you were to let go, who knows what might happen!
[MR TWIT *has a nasty idea*]

MR TWIT: Fear not, beloved! I'll never let you go!

MRS TWIT: There's enough pull here to take me to the moon!

MR TWIT: To the moon, my angel? What a thought!
[*He lets go of her ankles*]
[MRS TWIT *begins to rise. She climbs on the table*]

MRS TWIT: Oooh! Aaah! Help! Help!

MR TWIT: Goodbye, you old hag! Goodbye for ever!
[MRS TWIT *rises higher. And higher.* MR TWIT *freezes, waving goodbye. The* NARRATOR *steps in*]

NARRATOR: But we can't end our story like this! That wouldn't be fair! Mr and Mrs Twit are as nasty as each other. They deserve each other. Mr Twit cannot be allowed to win! Bring on the Birds!
[*The puppeteers enter, carrying the* BIRDS, *who fly around*]

[*Then, in the nick of time, they fly up and, with their beaks, begin to burst the balloons. Slowly, gracefully,* MRS TWIT *descends. She lands right on top of* MR TWIT. *They collapse in a heap. They struggle up, and* MRS TWIT *turns on* MR TWIT. *The* BIRDS *stay to watch*]

MRS TWIT: You nasty . . . loathsome . . . horrible . . . rotten . . . stinking . . . monstrous . . . Twit! I'll get you! You'll pay for that! I'll make you suffer! Come back! Come back!
[MR TWIT, *terrified, makes his escape—possibly through the audience—chased by* MRS TWIT *waving her walking stick at him*]

MR TWIT: You frazzled old fool!

MRS TWIT: You grizzly old grunion!

MR TWIT: You frumptious old freak!

MRS TWIT: You troggy old turnip!

MR TWIT: You maggoty old monkfish!

MRS TWIT: You filthy old frumpet!

MR TWIT: You mangy old mongoose!

MRS TWIT: You whiskery old warthog!

MR TWIT: I'll swish you to a swazzle!

MRS TWIT: I'll swash you to a swizzle!

MR TWIT: I'll gnash you to a gnozzle!

MRS TWIT: I'll gnosh you to a gnazzle!
    [*The* TWITS *exit*]

NARRATOR: A fair ending, if not a happy one!
    [*Curtain down*]

**READ ALL OF THESE WONDERFUL BOOKS FROM
THE WORLD'S NO. 1 STORYTELLER,**

Roald Dahl!

The BFG

Boy: Tales of Childhood

Charlie and the Chocolate Factory

Charlie and the Great Glass Elevator

Danny the Champion of the World

Dirty Beasts

The Enormous Crocodile

Esio Trot

Fantastic Mr. Fox

George's Marvelous Medicine

The Giraffe and the Pelly and Me

Going Solo

James and the Giant Peach

The Magic Finger

Matilda

The Minpins

*The Missing Golden Ticket
and Other Splendiferous Secrets*

Roald Dahl's Revolting Rhymes

The Twits

The Vicar of Nibbleswicke

The Witches

The Wonderful Story of Henry Sugar